50 Keto-Diet Recipes for Home

By: Kelly Johnson

Table of Contents

- Bacon and Cheese Egg Muffins
- Cauliflower Mac and Cheese
- Avocado and Bacon Stuffed Mushrooms
- Zucchini Noodles with Pesto
- Garlic Butter Steak Bites
- Keto Chicken Alfredo
- Spinach and Feta Stuffed Chicken Breast
- Creamy Broccoli Soup
- Coconut Flour Pancakes
- Lemon Garlic Shrimp Skewers
- Eggplant Lasagna
- Cheesy Cauliflower Casserole
- Greek Salad with Grilled Chicken
- Almond Flour Bread
- Keto Taco Salad
- Parmesan Crusted Salmon
- Beef and Broccoli Stir-Fry
- Creamy Tuscan Chicken
- Buffalo Chicken Lettuce Wraps
- Keto Chocolate Avocado Mousse
- Cauliflower Fried Rice
- Keto Meatballs with Marinara Sauce
- Spinach and Artichoke Stuffed Portobello Mushrooms
- Chicken Caesar Salad with Homemade Dressing
- Cheesy Bacon Brussels Sprouts
- Keto Pizza with Fathead Dough
- Coconut Curry Chicken
- Stuffed Bell Peppers with Ground Turkey and Cheese
- Keto Chocolate Chip Cookies
- Creamy Garlic Parmesan Shrimp
- Taco Stuffed Avocados
- Spaghetti Squash Carbonara
- Bacon-Wrapped Asparagus
- Keto Butter Chicken
- Broccoli Cheddar Soup

- Keto Cheeseburger Casserole
- Creamy Lemon Garlic Chicken
- Avocado Tuna Salad
- Almond Flour Blueberry Muffins
- Bacon-Wrapped Jalapeno Poppers
- Keto Chicken Salad Lettuce Wraps
- Cheesy Cauliflower Breadsticks
- Grilled Lemon Herb Chicken
- Keto Chocolate Peanut Butter Fat Bombs
- Creamy Mushroom Risotto
- Sausage and Pepperoni Cauliflower Pizza Casserole
- Lemon Butter Salmon
- Chicken Bacon Ranch Casserole
- Keto Strawberry Cheesecake Bites
- Spicy Thai Coconut Soup

Bacon and Cheese Egg Muffins

Ingredients:

- 6 large eggs
- 1/4 cup heavy cream (or milk of choice)
- Salt and pepper to taste
- 4 slices bacon, cooked and crumbled
- 1/2 cup shredded cheddar cheese
- 2 tablespoons chopped fresh chives or green onions (optional)

Instructions:

1. Preheat your oven to 350°F (175°C). Grease a muffin tin or line it with silicone muffin liners.
2. In a large mixing bowl, whisk together the eggs, heavy cream (or milk), salt, and pepper until well combined.
3. Stir in the crumbled bacon, shredded cheddar cheese, and chopped chives or green onions (if using) into the egg mixture.
4. Pour the egg mixture evenly into the prepared muffin tin, filling each cup about 3/4 full.
5. Bake in the preheated oven for 18-20 minutes, or until the egg muffins are set and slightly golden on top.
6. Remove the muffin tin from the oven and let the egg muffins cool for a few minutes before removing them from the tin.
7. Serve the bacon and cheese egg muffins warm, and enjoy!

These egg muffins can be stored in an airtight container in the refrigerator for up to 3 days. They're perfect for meal prep or for a quick and easy breakfast on the go.

Cauliflower Mac and Cheese

Ingredients:

- 1 large head of cauliflower, cut into florets
- 2 tablespoons butter
- 2 tablespoons all-purpose flour (or almond flour for a gluten-free option)
- 2 cups milk (any type you prefer)
- 2 cups shredded sharp cheddar cheese
- 1/2 cup grated Parmesan cheese
- 1 teaspoon Dijon mustard
- 1/2 teaspoon garlic powder
- Salt and pepper to taste
- Optional toppings: breadcrumbs, chopped parsley, or crispy bacon bits

Instructions:

1. Preheat your oven to 375°F (190°C). Grease a baking dish or casserole dish with butter or cooking spray.
2. Steam the cauliflower florets until they are tender but still slightly firm, about 5-7 minutes. Drain well and set aside.
3. In a large saucepan, melt the butter over medium heat. Add the flour and whisk continuously until it forms a smooth paste, about 1-2 minutes.
4. Gradually pour in the milk while whisking constantly to prevent lumps from forming. Continue to cook and stir until the mixture thickens, about 3-4 minutes.
5. Stir in the shredded cheddar cheese, grated Parmesan cheese, Dijon mustard, garlic powder, salt, and pepper until the cheese is melted and the sauce is smooth and creamy.
6. Add the steamed cauliflower florets to the cheese sauce and stir until they are evenly coated.
7. Transfer the cauliflower and cheese mixture to the prepared baking dish, spreading it out evenly.
8. If desired, sprinkle breadcrumbs on top of the cauliflower mixture for a crunchy topping.
9. Bake in the preheated oven for 20-25 minutes, or until the cheese is bubbly and golden brown on top.
10. Remove the cauliflower mac and cheese from the oven and let it cool for a few minutes before serving.

11. Garnish with chopped parsley or crispy bacon bits, if desired.
12. Serve hot and enjoy your delicious cauliflower mac and cheese!

This dish is creamy, cheesy, and packed with flavor, making it a favorite among both kids and adults. It's a great way to sneak in some extra veggies while still enjoying a classic comfort food.

Avocado and Bacon Stuffed Mushrooms

Ingredients:

- 12 large mushrooms, stems removed and cleaned
- 1 ripe avocado
- 4 slices of bacon, cooked and crumbled
- 1/4 cup grated Parmesan cheese
- 2 tablespoons chopped fresh cilantro or parsley
- 1 clove garlic, minced
- 1 tablespoon lime juice
- Salt and pepper to taste
- Optional garnish: chopped green onions or additional grated Parmesan cheese

Instructions:

1. Preheat your oven to 375°F (190°C). Line a baking sheet with parchment paper or aluminum foil.
2. In a medium mixing bowl, mash the avocado with a fork until smooth.
3. Stir in the crumbled bacon, grated Parmesan cheese, chopped cilantro or parsley, minced garlic, lime juice, salt, and pepper until well combined.
4. Place the cleaned mushrooms on the prepared baking sheet, cavity side up.
5. Spoon the avocado and bacon mixture into the cavity of each mushroom, dividing it evenly among them.
6. Sprinkle additional grated Parmesan cheese on top of each stuffed mushroom, if desired.
7. Bake in the preheated oven for 15-20 minutes, or until the mushrooms are tender and the filling is heated through.
8. Remove the stuffed mushrooms from the oven and let them cool for a few minutes before serving.
9. Garnish with chopped green onions or additional grated Parmesan cheese, if desired.
10. Serve the avocado and bacon stuffed mushrooms warm and enjoy as a tasty appetizer or snack!

These stuffed mushrooms are creamy, savory, and full of delicious flavors. They're perfect for parties, gatherings, or whenever you're craving a satisfying and flavorful bite.

Zucchini Noodles with Pesto

Ingredients:

For the zucchini noodles:

- 4 medium zucchini
- Salt to taste

For the pesto:

- 2 cups fresh basil leaves, packed
- 1/2 cup grated Parmesan cheese
- 1/2 cup pine nuts or walnuts
- 2 cloves garlic, minced
- 1/2 cup extra virgin olive oil
- Salt and pepper to taste

Optional toppings:

- Cherry tomatoes, halved
- Grated Parmesan cheese
- Fresh basil leaves
- Red pepper flakes

Instructions:

1. Prepare the zucchini noodles using a spiralizer or julienne peeler. If using a spiralizer, follow the manufacturer's instructions. If using a julienne peeler, run the peeler along the length of each zucchini to create long, thin noodles. Place the zucchini noodles in a colander and sprinkle with salt. Let them sit for about 10-15 minutes to release excess moisture. Afterward, pat the noodles dry with paper towels.
2. In a food processor or blender, combine the fresh basil leaves, grated Parmesan cheese, pine nuts or walnuts, minced garlic, salt, and pepper. Pulse until the ingredients are finely chopped.

3. With the food processor or blender running, slowly drizzle in the extra virgin olive oil until the pesto reaches your desired consistency. You may need to scrape down the sides of the bowl with a spatula to ensure all the ingredients are well combined.
4. Taste the pesto and adjust the seasoning as needed with salt and pepper.
5. In a large skillet, heat a small amount of olive oil over medium heat. Add the zucchini noodles to the skillet and sauté for 2-3 minutes, or until they are just tender.
6. Add the pesto to the skillet with the zucchini noodles, tossing to coat the noodles evenly with the pesto. Cook for an additional minute or until the pesto is heated through.
7. Serve the zucchini noodles with pesto immediately, garnished with cherry tomatoes, grated Parmesan cheese, fresh basil leaves, and red pepper flakes, if desired.
8. Enjoy your delicious zucchini noodles with pesto as a light and flavorful meal!

This dish is versatile, so feel free to customize it with your favorite toppings or add-ins. It's a great way to enjoy a healthy and satisfying meal that's low in carbs and packed with flavor.

Garlic Butter Steak Bites

Ingredients:

- 1 pound sirloin steak, cut into bite-sized cubes
- Salt and pepper to taste
- 2 tablespoons olive oil
- 4 tablespoons unsalted butter
- 4 cloves garlic, minced
- 1 tablespoon chopped fresh parsley (optional)
- Lemon wedges for serving (optional)

Instructions:

1. Season the steak cubes with salt and pepper to taste.
2. Heat the olive oil in a large skillet over medium-high heat until shimmering.
3. Add the steak cubes to the skillet in a single layer, making sure not to overcrowd the pan. Cook for 2-3 minutes without stirring to allow the steak to sear and develop a golden brown crust.
4. Flip the steak cubes and continue to cook for an additional 2-3 minutes, or until they are cooked to your desired level of doneness. Remove the steak from the skillet and transfer it to a plate. Cover loosely with foil to keep warm.
5. Reduce the heat to medium-low and add the butter to the skillet. Once the butter has melted, add the minced garlic and cook for 1-2 minutes, stirring frequently, until fragrant and golden brown. Be careful not to burn the garlic.
6. Return the cooked steak cubes to the skillet and toss them in the garlic butter sauce until they are evenly coated.
7. Sprinkle chopped fresh parsley over the steak bites, if using, and toss to combine.
8. Remove the skillet from the heat and transfer the garlic butter steak bites to a serving dish.
9. Serve the steak bites hot, garnished with lemon wedges for squeezing over the top, if desired.
10. Enjoy your delicious garlic butter steak bites as a flavorful appetizer or main course!

These steak bites are tender, juicy, and packed with savory garlic butter flavor. They're sure to be a hit with family and friends at any gathering or dinner table.

Keto Chicken Alfredo

Ingredients:

- 1 pound boneless, skinless chicken breasts, cut into bite-sized pieces
- Salt and pepper to taste
- 2 tablespoons olive oil
- 4 cloves garlic, minced
- 1 cup heavy cream
- 1/2 cup grated Parmesan cheese
- 2 tablespoons cream cheese
- 1 teaspoon garlic powder
- 1 teaspoon Italian seasoning
- 8 ounces cooked fettuccine or other low-carb pasta alternative (such as zucchini noodles or shirataki noodles)
- Chopped fresh parsley for garnish (optional)

Instructions:

1. Season the chicken pieces with salt and pepper to taste.
2. Heat the olive oil in a large skillet over medium-high heat. Add the seasoned chicken to the skillet and cook for 5-6 minutes, or until browned and cooked through. Remove the chicken from the skillet and set aside.
3. In the same skillet, add the minced garlic and cook for 1-2 minutes, until fragrant.
4. Reduce the heat to medium-low and pour in the heavy cream, stirring to scrape up any browned bits from the bottom of the skillet.
5. Stir in the grated Parmesan cheese, cream cheese, garlic powder, and Italian seasoning until the cheese is melted and the sauce is smooth and creamy.
6. Return the cooked chicken to the skillet and toss it in the Alfredo sauce until evenly coated. Cook for an additional 2-3 minutes to heat through.
7. Meanwhile, cook the fettuccine or low-carb pasta alternative according to the package instructions. Drain well.
8. Add the cooked pasta to the skillet with the chicken Alfredo sauce, tossing to combine.
9. Cook for an additional minute or until the pasta is heated through and coated in the sauce.
10. Remove the skillet from the heat and garnish the keto chicken Alfredo with chopped fresh parsley, if desired.

11. Serve hot and enjoy your delicious and satisfying low-carb meal!

This keto chicken Alfredo is creamy, indulgent, and perfect for anyone following a ketogenic diet or looking for a low-carb pasta alternative. It's a comforting and flavorful dish that's sure to become a favorite!

Spinach and Feta Stuffed Chicken Breast

Ingredients:

- 4 boneless, skinless chicken breasts
- Salt and pepper to taste
- 2 cups fresh spinach leaves, chopped
- 1/2 cup crumbled feta cheese
- 2 cloves garlic, minced
- 1 tablespoon olive oil
- 1 teaspoon dried oregano
- 1 teaspoon dried thyme
- 1/2 teaspoon paprika
- Toothpicks or kitchen twine (optional)

Instructions:

1. Preheat your oven to 375°F (190°C).
2. Use a sharp knife to carefully cut a pocket into each chicken breast. Be careful not to cut all the way through. Season the inside of each pocket with salt and pepper to taste.
3. In a skillet, heat the olive oil over medium heat. Add the minced garlic and cook for 1-2 minutes, until fragrant.
4. Add the chopped spinach to the skillet and cook for 2-3 minutes, until wilted. Remove from heat and let it cool slightly.
5. In a mixing bowl, combine the cooked spinach, crumbled feta cheese, dried oregano, dried thyme, and paprika. Stir until well mixed.
6. Stuff each chicken breast with the spinach and feta mixture, dividing it evenly among them. If necessary, use toothpicks or kitchen twine to secure the openings.
7. Season the outside of each stuffed chicken breast with additional salt and pepper, if desired.
8. Place the stuffed chicken breasts in a baking dish or on a baking sheet lined with parchment paper.
9. Bake in the preheated oven for 25-30 minutes, or until the chicken is cooked through and the juices run clear. The internal temperature of the chicken should reach 165°F (75°C).

10. Remove the stuffed chicken breasts from the oven and let them rest for a few minutes before serving.
11. Serve hot and enjoy your delicious spinach and feta stuffed chicken breast!

This dish is flavorful, juicy, and packed with protein and nutrients. It's perfect for serving with your favorite side dishes, such as roasted vegetables, mashed potatoes, or a simple salad.

Creamy Broccoli Soup

Ingredients:

- 4 cups fresh broccoli florets
- 1 tablespoon olive oil
- 1 small onion, chopped
- 2 cloves garlic, minced
- 4 cups vegetable or chicken broth
- 1 cup heavy cream or half-and-half
- Salt and pepper to taste
- Optional toppings: grated cheddar cheese, crumbled bacon, chopped chives, or sour cream

Instructions:

1. In a large pot, heat the olive oil over medium heat. Add the chopped onion and cook for 3-4 minutes, until softened.
2. Add the minced garlic to the pot and cook for an additional minute, until fragrant.
3. Add the broccoli florets to the pot and stir to combine with the onion and garlic.
4. Pour the vegetable or chicken broth into the pot, ensuring that the broccoli is submerged. Bring the mixture to a boil, then reduce the heat to low. Cover and simmer for about 15 minutes, or until the broccoli is tender.
5. Use an immersion blender to puree the soup until smooth. Alternatively, transfer the soup in batches to a blender and blend until smooth. Be careful when blending hot liquids.
6. Return the pureed soup to the pot over low heat. Stir in the heavy cream or half-and-half until well combined. Season with salt and pepper to taste.
7. Continue to cook the soup for an additional 5-10 minutes, stirring occasionally, to heat through and allow the flavors to meld together.
8. Remove the soup from the heat and ladle it into bowls.
9. Serve the creamy broccoli soup hot, garnished with grated cheddar cheese, crumbled bacon, chopped chives, or a dollop of sour cream, if desired.
10. Enjoy your comforting and delicious creamy broccoli soup!

This soup is rich, creamy, and packed with the flavor of fresh broccoli. It's perfect for lunch or dinner, and you can customize it with your favorite toppings for added texture and flavor.

Coconut Flour Pancakes

Ingredients:

- 1/4 cup coconut flour
- 1/2 teaspoon baking powder
- Pinch of salt
- 4 large eggs
- 1/4 cup coconut milk or almond milk
- 1 tablespoon coconut oil, melted
- 1 tablespoon honey or maple syrup (optional)
- 1/2 teaspoon vanilla extract

Instructions:

1. In a medium bowl, whisk together the coconut flour, baking powder, and salt until well combined.
2. In a separate bowl, beat the eggs until frothy. Add the coconut milk, melted coconut oil, honey or maple syrup (if using), and vanilla extract, and whisk until smooth.
3. Pour the wet ingredients into the dry ingredients and stir until just combined. Let the batter sit for a few minutes to allow the coconut flour to absorb the liquid and thicken.
4. Heat a non-stick skillet or griddle over medium heat. Lightly grease the surface with coconut oil or cooking spray.
5. Once the skillet is hot, pour about 1/4 cup of batter onto the skillet for each pancake. Use the back of a spoon to spread the batter into a round shape, if necessary.
6. Cook the pancakes for 2-3 minutes, or until bubbles form on the surface and the edges begin to look set.
7. Carefully flip the pancakes and cook for an additional 1-2 minutes on the other side, until golden brown and cooked through.
8. Repeat with the remaining batter, greasing the skillet as needed between batches.
9. Serve the coconut flour pancakes warm, topped with your favorite toppings such as fresh fruit, maple syrup, honey, nut butter, or shredded coconut.
10. Enjoy your delicious and fluffy coconut flour pancakes!

These pancakes are light, fluffy, and subtly sweet, with a hint of coconut flavor. They're perfect for a leisurely weekend breakfast or brunch, and they're sure to become a new favorite in your recipe rotation.

Lemon Garlic Shrimp Skewers

Ingredients:

- 1 pound large shrimp, peeled and deveined
- 2 cloves garlic, minced
- Zest of 1 lemon
- Juice of 1 lemon
- 2 tablespoons olive oil
- 1 tablespoon chopped fresh parsley
- Salt and pepper to taste
- Wooden or metal skewers

Instructions:

1. If you're using wooden skewers, soak them in water for at least 30 minutes to prevent them from burning on the grill.
2. In a mixing bowl, combine the minced garlic, lemon zest, lemon juice, olive oil, chopped parsley, salt, and pepper. Stir until well combined.
3. Add the peeled and deveined shrimp to the bowl with the marinade, tossing to coat the shrimp evenly. Let the shrimp marinate in the refrigerator for at least 30 minutes, or up to 2 hours for maximum flavor.
4. Preheat your grill or broiler to medium-high heat.
5. Thread the marinated shrimp onto the skewers, leaving a little space between each shrimp.
6. If grilling, lightly oil the grill grates to prevent sticking. Place the shrimp skewers on the grill and cook for 2-3 minutes per side, or until the shrimp are pink and opaque.
7. If broiling, place the shrimp skewers on a broiler pan lined with aluminum foil. Broil for 2-3 minutes per side, or until the shrimp are pink and opaque.
8. Remove the shrimp skewers from the grill or broiler and transfer them to a serving platter.
9. Garnish the shrimp skewers with additional chopped parsley and lemon wedges, if desired.
10. Serve the lemon garlic shrimp skewers hot, and enjoy as a delicious appetizer or main course!

These shrimp skewers are juicy, flavorful, and perfect for a summer barbecue or weeknight dinner. They pair well with a variety of side dishes, such as rice, salad, or grilled vegetables.

Eggplant Lasagna

Ingredients:

- 2 large eggplants, sliced lengthwise into 1/4-inch thick slices
- Salt
- Olive oil
- 1 pound ground beef or Italian sausage (optional)
- 1 onion, finely chopped
- 3 cloves garlic, minced
- 1 can (28 ounces) crushed tomatoes
- 2 tablespoons tomato paste
- 1 teaspoon dried oregano
- 1 teaspoon dried basil
- 1/2 teaspoon dried thyme
- Salt and pepper to taste
- 2 cups ricotta cheese
- 1 cup grated Parmesan cheese
- 2 cups shredded mozzarella cheese
- Fresh basil leaves for garnish (optional)

Instructions:

1. Preheat your oven to 375°F (190°C). Grease a baking sheet with olive oil or non-stick cooking spray.
2. Place the eggplant slices on the prepared baking sheet in a single layer. Sprinkle salt over the slices and let them sit for about 10-15 minutes to draw out excess moisture.
3. Pat the eggplant slices dry with paper towels to remove the excess moisture. Brush both sides of the slices with olive oil.
4. Arrange the eggplant slices in a single layer on the baking sheet. Bake in the preheated oven for 15-20 minutes, or until the slices are tender and lightly golden brown. Remove from the oven and set aside.
5. In a large skillet, heat a drizzle of olive oil over medium heat. Add the ground beef or Italian sausage (if using) and cook until browned, breaking it up with a spoon. Remove any excess fat from the skillet.

6. Add the chopped onion to the skillet with the cooked meat and cook for 2-3 minutes, until softened. Add the minced garlic and cook for an additional minute, until fragrant.
7. Stir in the crushed tomatoes, tomato paste, dried oregano, dried basil, dried thyme, salt, and pepper. Bring the mixture to a simmer and cook for 10-15 minutes, stirring occasionally, until the sauce has thickened slightly. Remove from heat and set aside.
8. In a mixing bowl, combine the ricotta cheese and grated Parmesan cheese.
9. To assemble the lasagna, spread a thin layer of the meat sauce in the bottom of a 9x13-inch baking dish. Arrange a layer of baked eggplant slices on top of the sauce, overlapping slightly if necessary.
10. Spread half of the ricotta cheese mixture over the eggplant slices, followed by half of the remaining meat sauce. Sprinkle half of the shredded mozzarella cheese over the meat sauce.
11. Repeat the layers with the remaining eggplant slices, ricotta cheese mixture, meat sauce, and shredded mozzarella cheese.
12. Cover the baking dish with aluminum foil and bake in the preheated oven for 30 minutes.
13. Remove the foil and bake for an additional 15-20 minutes, or until the cheese is bubbly and lightly golden brown.
14. Remove the eggplant lasagna from the oven and let it cool for a few minutes before serving.
15. Garnish with fresh basil leaves, if desired.
16. Serve hot and enjoy your delicious and comforting eggplant lasagna!

This eggplant lasagna is rich, flavorful, and satisfying, making it a great option for a family dinner or gathering. Plus, it's a fantastic way to enjoy the flavors of lasagna while incorporating more vegetables into your meal.

Cheesy Cauliflower Casserole

Ingredients:

- 1 large head of cauliflower, cut into florets
- 2 tablespoons butter
- 2 tablespoons all-purpose flour (or almond flour for a gluten-free option)
- 1 cup milk
- 1 cup shredded cheddar cheese
- 1/2 cup grated Parmesan cheese
- 1 teaspoon garlic powder
- 1/2 teaspoon onion powder
- Salt and pepper to taste
- Optional toppings: chopped fresh parsley, crispy bacon bits, or breadcrumbs

Instructions:

1. Preheat your oven to 375°F (190°C). Grease a baking dish or casserole dish with butter or cooking spray.
2. Steam the cauliflower florets until they are tender but still slightly firm, about 5-7 minutes. Drain well and set aside.
3. In a medium saucepan, melt the butter over medium heat. Add the flour and whisk continuously until it forms a smooth paste, about 1-2 minutes.
4. Gradually pour in the milk while whisking constantly to prevent lumps from forming. Continue to cook and stir until the mixture thickens, about 3-4 minutes.
5. Stir in the shredded cheddar cheese, grated Parmesan cheese, garlic powder, onion powder, salt, and pepper until the cheese is melted and the sauce is smooth and creamy.
6. Add the steamed cauliflower florets to the cheese sauce and stir until they are evenly coated.
7. Transfer the cauliflower and cheese mixture to the prepared baking dish, spreading it out evenly.
8. If desired, sprinkle chopped fresh parsley, crispy bacon bits, or breadcrumbs on top of the cauliflower mixture for added flavor and texture.
9. Bake in the preheated oven for 20-25 minutes, or until the cheese is bubbly and golden brown on top.
10. Remove the cauliflower casserole from the oven and let it cool for a few minutes before serving.

11. Serve hot and enjoy your delicious and cheesy cauliflower casserole!

This dish is creamy, cheesy, and packed with flavor, making it a favorite among both kids and adults. It's a great way to enjoy cauliflower in a new and delicious way, and it pairs well with a variety of main dishes.

Greek Salad with Grilled Chicken

Ingredients:

For the grilled chicken:

- 2 boneless, skinless chicken breasts
- 2 tablespoons olive oil
- 1 tablespoon lemon juice
- 2 cloves garlic, minced
- 1 teaspoon dried oregano
- Salt and pepper to taste

For the salad:

- 4 cups mixed salad greens (such as romaine lettuce, spinach, and arugula)
- 1 cucumber, sliced
- 1 cup cherry tomatoes, halved
- 1/2 red onion, thinly sliced
- 1/2 cup Kalamata olives, pitted
- 1/2 cup crumbled feta cheese
- Optional toppings: sliced pepperoncini, chopped fresh parsley, or diced red bell pepper

For the dressing:

- 1/4 cup extra virgin olive oil
- 2 tablespoons red wine vinegar
- 1 clove garlic, minced
- 1 teaspoon dried oregano
- Salt and pepper to taste

Instructions:

1. In a shallow dish or resealable plastic bag, combine the olive oil, lemon juice, minced garlic, dried oregano, salt, and pepper. Add the chicken breasts and toss to coat. Marinate in the refrigerator for at least 30 minutes, or up to 4 hours.
2. Preheat your grill or grill pan to medium-high heat. Remove the chicken breasts from the marinade and discard any excess marinade. Grill the chicken for 6-8

minutes per side, or until cooked through and no longer pink in the center. Remove from the grill and let rest for a few minutes before slicing.
3. While the chicken is grilling, prepare the salad ingredients. In a large salad bowl, combine the mixed salad greens, sliced cucumber, halved cherry tomatoes, thinly sliced red onion, Kalamata olives, and crumbled feta cheese. Toss to combine.
4. In a small bowl, whisk together the extra virgin olive oil, red wine vinegar, minced garlic, dried oregano, salt, and pepper to make the dressing.
5. Add the sliced grilled chicken to the salad bowl. Drizzle the dressing over the salad and toss gently to coat.
6. Divide the Greek salad with grilled chicken among serving plates. Garnish with optional toppings such as sliced pepperoncini, chopped fresh parsley, or diced red bell pepper, if desired.
7. Serve immediately and enjoy your delicious and nutritious Greek salad with grilled chicken!

This salad is light, flavorful, and packed with protein and vegetables. It's perfect for a healthy and satisfying meal any day of the week.

Almond Flour Bread

Ingredients:

- 2 cups almond flour
- 1/4 cup flaxseed meal (optional, for added fiber)
- 1/4 cup psyllium husk powder (helps to bind the ingredients together)
- 1 teaspoon baking powder
- 1/2 teaspoon salt
- 4 large eggs
- 1/4 cup olive oil or melted butter
- 1/4 cup unsweetened almond milk or water
- 1 tablespoon apple cider vinegar (helps to activate the baking powder)

Instructions:

1. Preheat your oven to 350°F (175°C). Grease a 9x5-inch loaf pan with olive oil or line it with parchment paper.
2. In a large mixing bowl, whisk together the almond flour, flaxseed meal, psyllium husk powder, baking powder, and salt until well combined.
3. In a separate bowl, beat the eggs until frothy. Add the olive oil or melted butter, almond milk or water, and apple cider vinegar, and whisk until smooth.
4. Pour the wet ingredients into the dry ingredients and stir until a thick, sticky dough forms. The psyllium husk powder will absorb moisture and help bind the ingredients together.
5. Transfer the dough to the prepared loaf pan and smooth the top with a spatula.
6. Bake in the preheated oven for 40-45 minutes, or until the bread is golden brown and a toothpick inserted into the center comes out clean.
7. Remove the bread from the oven and let it cool in the pan for 10 minutes. Then, carefully transfer the bread to a wire rack to cool completely before slicing.
8. Once cooled, slice the almond flour bread into thick slices and serve.
9. Enjoy your delicious and nutritious almond flour bread with your favorite toppings, such as butter, nut butter, avocado, or cheese!

This bread is dense, moist, and has a slightly nutty flavor from the almond flour. It's perfect for sandwiches, toast, or simply enjoyed on its own as a tasty and satisfying snack. Plus, it's packed with protein and healthy fats, making it a great choice for anyone looking to add more nutrients to their diet.

Keto Taco Salad

Ingredients:

For the taco meat:

- 1 pound ground beef (or ground turkey or chicken)
- 1 tablespoon olive oil
- 1 small onion, chopped
- 2 cloves garlic, minced
- 1 tablespoon chili powder
- 1 teaspoon ground cumin
- 1/2 teaspoon paprika
- Salt and pepper to taste
- 1/4 cup water

For the salad:

- 4 cups chopped lettuce (such as romaine or iceberg)
- 1 cup cherry tomatoes, halved
- 1/2 cup shredded cheddar cheese
- 1/4 cup sliced black olives
- 1/4 cup diced red onion
- 1 avocado, diced
- Optional toppings: diced jalapeños, chopped cilantro, sour cream, or salsa

Instructions:

1. In a large skillet, heat the olive oil over medium heat. Add the chopped onion and minced garlic, and cook for 2-3 minutes until softened.
2. Add the ground beef to the skillet and cook, breaking it up with a spoon, until browned and cooked through.
3. Stir in the chili powder, ground cumin, paprika, salt, and pepper, and cook for an additional 1-2 minutes until fragrant.
4. Pour in the water and stir to combine. Simmer the taco meat for 5-10 minutes, or until the liquid has evaporated and the flavors have melded together. Remove from heat and set aside.

5. In a large salad bowl, layer the chopped lettuce, cherry tomatoes, shredded cheddar cheese, sliced black olives, diced red onion, and diced avocado.
6. Spoon the cooked taco meat over the salad ingredients.
7. Top the salad with optional toppings such as diced jalapeños, chopped cilantro, sour cream, or salsa.
8. Toss the salad gently to combine all the ingredients.
9. Serve immediately and enjoy your delicious keto taco salad!

This salad is hearty, flavorful, and perfect for a quick and satisfying meal. It's customizable with your favorite taco toppings and can be easily adapted to suit your taste preferences. Plus, it's low in carbs and high in protein, making it a great option for anyone following a keto or low-carb diet.

Parmesan Crusted Salmon

Ingredients:

- 4 salmon fillets (about 6 ounces each), skin removed
- Salt and pepper to taste
- 1/4 cup grated Parmesan cheese
- 2 tablespoons plain Greek yogurt or mayonnaise
- 1 tablespoon Dijon mustard
- 1 tablespoon lemon juice
- 1 teaspoon garlic powder
- 1 teaspoon dried parsley
- 1/4 cup almond flour or breadcrumbs (optional, for extra crust)

Instructions:

1. Preheat your oven to 400°F (200°C). Line a baking sheet with parchment paper or lightly grease it with olive oil.
2. Season the salmon fillets with salt and pepper to taste and place them on the prepared baking sheet.
3. In a small bowl, combine the grated Parmesan cheese, Greek yogurt or mayonnaise, Dijon mustard, lemon juice, garlic powder, and dried parsley. Stir until well combined.
4. Spread the Parmesan mixture evenly over the top of each salmon fillet, using the back of a spoon to coat the surface.
5. If using almond flour or breadcrumbs for extra crust, sprinkle them evenly over the Parmesan mixture on each salmon fillet.
6. Bake the salmon in the preheated oven for 12-15 minutes, or until the salmon is cooked through and flakes easily with a fork. The crust should be golden brown and crispy.
7. Remove the salmon from the oven and let it rest for a few minutes before serving.
8. Serve the Parmesan-crusted salmon hot, garnished with fresh lemon wedges and chopped parsley, if desired.
9. Enjoy your delicious and flavorful Parmesan-crusted salmon!

This dish is rich in protein, omega-3 fatty acids, and calcium from the salmon and Parmesan cheese. It's perfect for a quick weeknight dinner or a special occasion meal.

Serve it with your favorite side dishes, such as roasted vegetables, steamed greens, or a fresh salad, for a complete and nutritious meal.

Beef and Broccoli Stir-Fry

Ingredients:

For the beef marinade:

- 1 pound flank steak or sirloin steak, thinly sliced against the grain
- 2 tablespoons soy sauce
- 1 tablespoon cornstarch
- 1 tablespoon vegetable oil

For the stir-fry sauce:

- 1/4 cup soy sauce
- 2 tablespoons oyster sauce
- 2 tablespoons brown sugar
- 1 tablespoon rice vinegar or apple cider vinegar
- 2 cloves garlic, minced
- 1 teaspoon grated ginger
- 1/2 cup beef broth or water

For the stir-fry:

- 2 tablespoons vegetable oil, divided
- 4 cups broccoli florets
- 1 medium onion, thinly sliced
- Cooked rice or noodles for serving

Instructions:

1. In a medium bowl, combine the thinly sliced beef with 2 tablespoons of soy sauce, 1 tablespoon of cornstarch, and 1 tablespoon of vegetable oil. Stir until the beef is well coated. Let it marinate for at least 15-30 minutes, or up to overnight in the refrigerator.
2. In another bowl, whisk together the ingredients for the stir-fry sauce: 1/4 cup soy sauce, 2 tablespoons oyster sauce, 2 tablespoons brown sugar, 1 tablespoon vinegar, minced garlic, grated ginger, and beef broth or water. Set aside.
3. Heat 1 tablespoon of vegetable oil in a large skillet or wok over medium-high heat. Add the marinated beef in a single layer and cook for 1-2 minutes on each

side, until browned but still slightly pink in the center. Remove the beef from the skillet and set aside.
4. In the same skillet, add the remaining 1 tablespoon of vegetable oil. Add the broccoli florets and sliced onion, and stir-fry for 3-4 minutes, until the broccoli is crisp-tender.
5. Return the cooked beef to the skillet with the broccoli and onion. Pour the stir-fry sauce over the beef and vegetables, stirring to coat everything evenly.
6. Cook for an additional 2-3 minutes, until the sauce has thickened slightly and the beef is cooked through.
7. Remove the beef and broccoli stir-fry from the heat and serve immediately over cooked rice or noodles.
8. Enjoy your delicious and flavorful beef and broccoli stir-fry!

This dish is perfect for a quick weeknight dinner and can be customized with your favorite vegetables or protein. It's a great way to enjoy a healthy and satisfying meal that's packed with flavor.

Creamy Tuscan Chicken

Ingredients:

- 4 boneless, skinless chicken breasts
- Salt and pepper to taste
- 2 tablespoons olive oil
- 3 cloves garlic, minced
- 1 cup cherry tomatoes, halved
- 1 cup baby spinach leaves
- 1/2 cup sun-dried tomatoes, chopped
- 1 cup heavy cream
- 1/2 cup grated Parmesan cheese
- 1 teaspoon dried Italian seasoning
- Fresh basil leaves for garnish (optional)

Instructions:

1. Season the chicken breasts with salt and pepper to taste.
2. In a large skillet, heat the olive oil over medium-high heat. Add the seasoned chicken breasts to the skillet and cook for 6-7 minutes per side, or until golden brown and cooked through. Remove the chicken from the skillet and set aside.
3. In the same skillet, add the minced garlic and cook for 1-2 minutes, until fragrant.
4. Add the cherry tomatoes to the skillet and cook for 2-3 minutes, until they start to soften.
5. Stir in the baby spinach leaves and sun-dried tomatoes, and cook for an additional 1-2 minutes, until the spinach wilts.
6. Reduce the heat to medium-low and pour in the heavy cream, stirring to combine.
7. Stir in the grated Parmesan cheese and dried Italian seasoning until the cheese is melted and the sauce is smooth and creamy.
8. Return the cooked chicken breasts to the skillet, turning to coat them evenly in the creamy sauce.
9. Cook for an additional 2-3 minutes, until the chicken is heated through and the sauce has thickened slightly.
10. Remove the skillet from the heat and garnish the creamy Tuscan chicken with fresh basil leaves, if desired.
11. Serve hot and enjoy your delicious and flavorful creamy Tuscan chicken!

This dish pairs well with pasta, rice, or crusty bread for soaking up the creamy sauce. It's perfect for a special dinner or a cozy night in with loved ones.

Buffalo Chicken Lettuce Wraps

Ingredients:

For the buffalo chicken:

- 2 boneless, skinless chicken breasts
- Salt and pepper to taste
- 1/2 cup buffalo sauce (store-bought or homemade)
- 2 tablespoons butter, melted
- 1 tablespoon honey (optional, for sweetness)
- 1 teaspoon garlic powder
- 1 teaspoon onion powder
- 1/2 teaspoon paprika
- 1/4 teaspoon cayenne pepper (adjust to taste)
- 1/4 cup chopped green onions (optional, for garnish)

For the lettuce wraps:

- Large lettuce leaves (such as iceberg or romaine)
- Celery sticks, for serving
- Carrot sticks, for serving
- Ranch or blue cheese dressing, for dipping

Instructions:

1. Preheat your oven to 375°F (190°C). Grease a baking dish with cooking spray or olive oil.
2. Season the chicken breasts with salt and pepper to taste and place them in the prepared baking dish.
3. In a small bowl, whisk together the buffalo sauce, melted butter, honey (if using), garlic powder, onion powder, paprika, and cayenne pepper until well combined.
4. Pour the buffalo sauce mixture over the chicken breasts, making sure they are evenly coated.
5. Bake in the preheated oven for 25-30 minutes, or until the chicken is cooked through and reaches an internal temperature of 165°F (75°C).

6. Remove the chicken from the oven and let it cool for a few minutes. Then, shred the chicken using two forks.
7. To assemble the lettuce wraps, place a spoonful of the shredded buffalo chicken onto each lettuce leaf.
8. Top the buffalo chicken with chopped green onions, if desired.
9. Serve the buffalo chicken lettuce wraps with celery sticks, carrot sticks, and ranch or blue cheese dressing for dipping.
10. Enjoy your delicious and flavorful buffalo chicken lettuce wraps!

These lettuce wraps are perfect for a light lunch, appetizer, or even a healthy dinner option. They're easy to customize with your favorite toppings and can be made ahead of time for a quick and convenient meal.

Keto Chocolate Avocado Mousse

Ingredients:

- 2 ripe avocados
- 1/4 cup unsweetened cocoa powder
- 1/4 cup powdered erythritol or monk fruit sweetener
- 1 teaspoon vanilla extract
- Pinch of salt
- Optional toppings: whipped cream, berries, chopped nuts, or shaved chocolate

Instructions:

1. Cut the avocados in half and remove the pits. Scoop the avocado flesh into a blender or food processor.
2. Add the unsweetened cocoa powder, powdered erythritol or monk fruit sweetener, vanilla extract, and a pinch of salt to the blender or food processor.
3. Blend the ingredients until smooth and creamy, scraping down the sides of the blender or food processor as needed to ensure everything is well combined.
4. Taste the mousse and adjust the sweetness if necessary by adding more powdered sweetener, a little at a time, until desired sweetness is reached.
5. Transfer the chocolate avocado mousse to serving bowls or glasses.
6. Chill the mousse in the refrigerator for at least 30 minutes to allow it to firm up and develop the flavors.
7. Once chilled, top the mousse with optional toppings such as whipped cream, berries, chopped nuts, or shaved chocolate.
8. Serve and enjoy your delicious and creamy keto chocolate avocado mousse!

This dessert is rich, creamy, and satisfying, making it the perfect treat for anyone following a keto or low-carb diet. Plus, it's quick and easy to make, requiring just a few simple ingredients and minimal preparation time.

Cauliflower Fried Rice

Ingredients:

- 1 medium head cauliflower
- 2 tablespoons sesame oil or olive oil
- 2 cloves garlic, minced
- 1 small onion, finely chopped
- 2 carrots, diced
- 1 cup frozen peas and carrots, thawed
- 2 eggs, lightly beaten
- 3 tablespoons soy sauce or tamari
- 1 tablespoon rice vinegar (optional)
- Salt and pepper to taste
- Green onions, sliced, for garnish (optional)
- Sesame seeds, for garnish (optional)

Instructions:

1. Remove the core and leaves from the cauliflower head. Cut the cauliflower into florets and place them in a food processor. Pulse the cauliflower florets until they resemble rice grains. Alternatively, you can use a box grater to grate the cauliflower.
2. Heat 1 tablespoon of sesame oil or olive oil in a large skillet or wok over medium heat. Add the minced garlic and chopped onion, and sauté for 2-3 minutes until softened and fragrant.
3. Add the diced carrots to the skillet and cook for 3-4 minutes, until they start to soften.
4. Push the vegetables to one side of the skillet and add the remaining tablespoon of sesame oil or olive oil to the empty side. Pour the beaten eggs into the skillet and scramble them until cooked through.
5. Stir the scrambled eggs into the vegetables in the skillet.
6. Add the cauliflower rice to the skillet and stir to combine with the vegetables and eggs.
7. Drizzle the soy sauce or tamari over the cauliflower rice mixture. Add rice vinegar, if using. Stir well to evenly distribute the sauce.
8. Cook the cauliflower fried rice for 5-7 minutes, stirring occasionally, until the cauliflower rice is tender but not mushy.

9. Season with salt and pepper to taste.
10. Garnish the cauliflower fried rice with sliced green onions and sesame seeds, if desired.
11. Serve hot and enjoy your delicious and healthy cauliflower fried rice!

This dish is flavorful, satisfying, and packed with vegetables, making it a great option for a quick and nutritious meal. Plus, it's versatile and can be customized with your favorite protein or additional toppings, such as cooked chicken, shrimp, tofu, or extra vegetables.

Keto Meatballs with Marinara Sauce

Ingredients for Meatballs:

- 1 pound ground beef (you can also use ground turkey or chicken)
- 1/4 cup almond flour (or coconut flour for a nut-free option)
- 1/4 cup grated Parmesan cheese
- 1 large egg
- 2 cloves garlic, minced
- 1 teaspoon dried oregano
- 1 teaspoon dried basil
- 1/2 teaspoon salt
- 1/4 teaspoon black pepper
- 2 tablespoons olive oil (for frying)

Ingredients for Marinara Sauce:

- 1 tablespoon olive oil
- 1 small onion, finely chopped
- 2 cloves garlic, minced
- 1 (14-ounce) can crushed tomatoes
- 1 teaspoon dried oregano
- 1 teaspoon dried basil
- Salt and pepper to taste

Instructions:

1. Preheat your oven to 375°F (190°C).
2. In a large mixing bowl, combine the ground beef, almond flour, Parmesan cheese, egg, minced garlic, dried oregano, dried basil, salt, and black pepper. Mix until all ingredients are well combined.
3. Roll the mixture into meatballs, about 1 to 1.5 inches in diameter, and place them on a baking sheet lined with parchment paper.
4. Heat 2 tablespoons of olive oil in a large skillet over medium-high heat. Once hot, add the meatballs in batches, making sure not to overcrowd the skillet. Cook for 2-3 minutes on each side, or until browned. Transfer the browned meatballs to a plate lined with paper towels to drain any excess oil.

5. Once all the meatballs are browned, transfer them to the preheated oven and bake for 10-15 minutes, or until they are cooked through.
6. While the meatballs are baking, prepare the marinara sauce. In the same skillet used for browning the meatballs, heat 1 tablespoon of olive oil over medium heat. Add the finely chopped onion and cook for 3-4 minutes, until softened.
7. Add the minced garlic to the skillet and cook for an additional 1 minute, until fragrant.
8. Stir in the crushed tomatoes, dried oregano, and dried basil. Season with salt and pepper to taste. Bring the sauce to a simmer and cook for 5-10 minutes, stirring occasionally, to allow the flavors to meld together.
9. Once the meatballs are cooked through, remove them from the oven and add them to the marinara sauce. Gently stir to coat the meatballs in the sauce.
10. Serve the keto meatballs with marinara sauce hot, garnished with fresh basil or grated Parmesan cheese if desired.

Enjoy your delicious and keto-friendly meatballs with marinara sauce! They're perfect for a satisfying low-carb meal.

Spinach and Artichoke Stuffed Portobello Mushrooms

Ingredients:

- 4 large portobello mushrooms
- 2 tablespoons olive oil
- 2 cloves garlic, minced
- 2 cups fresh spinach, chopped
- 1 (14 oz) can artichoke hearts, drained and chopped
- 1/2 cup grated Parmesan cheese
- 1/2 cup shredded mozzarella cheese
- 1/4 cup cream cheese
- Salt and pepper to taste
- Fresh parsley, chopped (for garnish)

Instructions:

1. Preheat your oven to 375°F (190°C). Line a baking sheet with parchment paper or aluminum foil.
2. Clean the portobello mushrooms by wiping them with a damp paper towel. Remove the stems and gills from the mushrooms and discard.
3. Place the mushrooms on the prepared baking sheet, gill side up. Drizzle the mushrooms with olive oil and season with salt and pepper.
4. In a skillet, heat 1 tablespoon of olive oil over medium heat. Add the minced garlic and cook for 1-2 minutes, until fragrant.
5. Add the chopped spinach to the skillet and cook until wilted, about 2-3 minutes.
6. Stir in the chopped artichoke hearts and cook for an additional 2 minutes.
7. Remove the skillet from the heat and stir in the grated Parmesan cheese, shredded mozzarella cheese, and cream cheese until well combined. Season with salt and pepper to taste.
8. Spoon the spinach and artichoke mixture into each portobello mushroom cap, dividing it evenly among them.
9. Place the stuffed mushrooms in the preheated oven and bake for 15-20 minutes, or until the mushrooms are tender and the cheese is melted and bubbly.
10. Remove the stuffed mushrooms from the oven and garnish with chopped fresh parsley.
11. Serve the spinach and artichoke stuffed portobello mushrooms hot as a delicious appetizer or side dish.

Enjoy your flavorful and satisfying Spinach and Artichoke Stuffed Portobello Mushrooms! They make a perfect dish for any occasion, and they're sure to impress your guests with their delicious taste and beautiful presentation.

Chicken Caesar Salad with Homemade Dressing

Ingredients:

For the Caesar Dressing:

- 1/2 cup mayonnaise
- 2 cloves garlic, minced
- 2 anchovy fillets, minced (optional)
- 2 tablespoons freshly squeezed lemon juice
- 1 tablespoon Dijon mustard
- 1 teaspoon Worcestershire sauce
- 1/4 cup grated Parmesan cheese
- Salt and pepper to taste

For the Salad:

- 2 boneless, skinless chicken breasts
- Salt and pepper to taste
- 1 tablespoon olive oil
- 1 large head of romaine lettuce, chopped
- 1 cup croutons (homemade or store-bought)
- 1/4 cup grated Parmesan cheese
- Lemon wedges for serving (optional)

Instructions:

1. Preheat your grill or grill pan to medium-high heat.
2. Season the chicken breasts with salt and pepper to taste. Drizzle with olive oil and rub to coat evenly.
3. Grill the chicken breasts for 6-8 minutes per side, or until cooked through and no longer pink in the center. Remove from the grill and let rest for a few minutes before slicing.
4. While the chicken is cooking, prepare the Caesar dressing. In a small bowl, whisk together the mayonnaise, minced garlic, minced anchovy fillets (if using), lemon juice, Dijon mustard, Worcestershire sauce, and grated Parmesan cheese until

smooth and well combined. Season with salt and pepper to taste. If the dressing is too thick, you can thin it out with a little water or more lemon juice.
5. Once the chicken has rested, slice it into thin strips.
6. In a large salad bowl, combine the chopped romaine lettuce and croutons. Add the sliced grilled chicken on top.
7. Drizzle the Caesar dressing over the salad, tossing gently to coat everything evenly.
8. Sprinkle the grated Parmesan cheese over the salad as a garnish.
9. Serve the Chicken Caesar salad immediately, garnished with lemon wedges if desired.
10. Enjoy your delicious homemade Chicken Caesar salad!

This salad is perfect for a light and satisfying meal, and the homemade dressing adds a fresh and flavorful touch. Feel free to customize the salad with additional toppings such as cherry tomatoes, bacon bits, or avocado slices, according to your preference.

Cheesy Bacon Brussels Sprouts

Ingredients:

- 1 pound Brussels sprouts, trimmed and halved
- 6 slices bacon, chopped
- 1/2 onion, finely chopped
- 2 cloves garlic, minced
- 1/2 cup chicken broth or vegetable broth
- 1/2 cup heavy cream
- 1 cup shredded cheddar cheese
- Salt and pepper to taste
- Chopped parsley or green onions for garnish (optional)

Instructions:

1. In a large skillet or frying pan, cook the chopped bacon over medium heat until it becomes crispy and browned. Remove the cooked bacon from the pan and place it on a paper towel-lined plate to drain excess grease. Leave about 1 tablespoon of bacon grease in the pan.
2. In the same skillet, add the finely chopped onion and minced garlic. Cook for 2-3 minutes until softened and fragrant.
3. Add the halved Brussels sprouts to the skillet and cook for about 5 minutes, stirring occasionally, until they start to brown and caramelize.
4. Pour the chicken broth or vegetable broth into the skillet and cover with a lid. Allow the Brussels sprouts to steam for about 5-7 minutes, or until they are tender but still slightly crisp.
5. Remove the lid and stir in the heavy cream. Let the mixture simmer for a few minutes until the cream has thickened slightly.
6. Stir in the shredded cheddar cheese and cooked bacon until the cheese is melted and the sauce is creamy. Season with salt and pepper to taste.
7. Remove the skillet from the heat and transfer the cheesy bacon Brussels sprouts to a serving dish.
8. Garnish with chopped parsley or green onions, if desired, before serving.
9. Serve hot and enjoy your delicious cheesy bacon Brussels sprouts as a side dish to accompany your favorite main course!

This dish is perfect for special occasions or everyday meals, and it's sure to be a hit with Brussels sprout lovers and bacon enthusiasts alike.

Keto Pizza with Fathead Dough

Ingredients for Fathead Dough:

- 1 1/2 cups shredded mozzarella cheese
- 2 tablespoons cream cheese
- 1 1/2 cups almond flour
- 2 tablespoons psyllium husk powder (optional, for extra texture and fiber)
- 1 teaspoon baking powder
- 1/2 teaspoon garlic powder
- 1/2 teaspoon Italian seasoning
- 1 large egg
- Salt to taste

Ingredients for Pizza Toppings:

- 1/2 cup sugar-free pizza sauce or marinara sauce
- 1 1/2 cups shredded mozzarella cheese (or your favorite cheese blend)
- Your favorite pizza toppings (e.g., pepperoni, cooked sausage, bell peppers, onions, mushrooms, olives, etc.)
- Fresh basil leaves, chopped (optional, for garnish)

Instructions:

1. Preheat your oven to 425°F (220°C). Line a baking sheet with parchment paper or a silicone baking mat.
2. In a microwave-safe bowl, combine the shredded mozzarella cheese and cream cheese. Microwave in 30-second intervals, stirring in between, until the cheeses are melted and well combined.
3. In a separate bowl, whisk together the almond flour, psyllium husk powder (if using), baking powder, garlic powder, Italian seasoning, and salt.
4. Add the dry ingredients to the melted cheese mixture along with the egg. Mix until a dough forms. If the dough is too sticky, you can wet your hands with water or lightly oil them to prevent sticking.
5. Transfer the dough to the prepared baking sheet. Place another sheet of parchment paper on top of the dough and use a rolling pin to roll it out into a thin crust, about 1/4 inch thick.

6. Remove the top parchment paper and bake the crust in the preheated oven for 8-10 minutes, or until it is lightly golden brown and set.
7. Remove the crust from the oven and spread the pizza sauce evenly over the surface. Sprinkle the shredded mozzarella cheese over the sauce, then add your desired pizza toppings.
8. Return the pizza to the oven and bake for an additional 8-10 minutes, or until the cheese is melted and bubbly and the crust is golden brown.
9. Remove the pizza from the oven and let it cool for a few minutes before slicing.
10. Garnish with chopped fresh basil leaves, if desired, before serving.
11. Slice and enjoy your delicious keto pizza with fathead dough!

This recipe makes a fantastic low-carb pizza that's perfect for anyone following a ketogenic diet or looking to reduce their carb intake without sacrificing flavor. Feel free to customize the toppings to suit your taste preferences!

Coconut Curry Chicken

Ingredients:

- 1 1/2 pounds boneless, skinless chicken breasts or thighs, cut into bite-sized pieces
- 2 tablespoons coconut oil or vegetable oil
- 1 onion, finely chopped
- 3 cloves garlic, minced
- 1 tablespoon grated ginger
- 2 tablespoons curry powder
- 1 teaspoon ground turmeric
- 1 teaspoon ground cumin
- 1/2 teaspoon ground coriander
- 1/2 teaspoon paprika
- 1/4 teaspoon cayenne pepper (adjust to taste)
- 1 can (14 ounces) coconut milk
- 1 cup chicken broth
- 2 tablespoons tomato paste
- 2 tablespoons soy sauce or tamari (for gluten-free)
- 1 tablespoon brown sugar or honey (optional, for sweetness)
- Salt and pepper to taste
- Fresh cilantro, chopped, for garnish (optional)
- Cooked rice or naan bread, for serving

Instructions:

1. Heat the coconut oil or vegetable oil in a large skillet or Dutch oven over medium heat. Add the chopped onion and cook for 3-4 minutes until softened and translucent.
2. Add the minced garlic and grated ginger to the skillet and cook for an additional 1-2 minutes until fragrant.
3. Stir in the curry powder, ground turmeric, ground cumin, ground coriander, paprika, and cayenne pepper. Cook for 1-2 minutes until the spices are toasted and fragrant.
4. Add the bite-sized chicken pieces to the skillet and cook until browned on all sides, about 5-7 minutes.

5. Pour in the coconut milk, chicken broth, tomato paste, soy sauce or tamari, and brown sugar or honey (if using). Stir to combine and bring the mixture to a simmer.
6. Reduce the heat to low and let the coconut curry chicken simmer gently for 15-20 minutes, stirring occasionally, until the chicken is cooked through and the sauce has thickened slightly.
7. Taste the curry and adjust the seasoning with salt and pepper as needed.
8. Remove the skillet from the heat and garnish the coconut curry chicken with chopped fresh cilantro, if desired.
9. Serve hot over cooked rice or with naan bread for soaking up the delicious sauce.
10. Enjoy your flavorful and aromatic coconut curry chicken!

This dish is perfect for a cozy weeknight dinner or for entertaining guests. It's packed with flavor and pairs well with a variety of side dishes, such as steamed vegetables, cauliflower rice, or quinoa. Feel free to customize the spice level and ingredients to suit your taste preferences.

Stuffed Bell Peppers with Ground Turkey and Cheese

Ingredients:

- 4 large bell peppers (any color), halved and seeds removed
- 1 pound ground turkey (or ground chicken)
- 1 tablespoon olive oil
- 1 small onion, finely chopped
- 2 cloves garlic, minced
- 1 teaspoon Italian seasoning
- 1/2 teaspoon paprika
- Salt and pepper to taste
- 1 cup cooked rice (white or brown)
- 1 cup shredded cheese (cheddar, mozzarella, or your favorite melting cheese)
- Fresh parsley or green onions, chopped, for garnish (optional)

Instructions:

1. Preheat your oven to 375°F (190°C). Arrange the halved bell peppers in a baking dish, cut side up.
2. In a large skillet, heat the olive oil over medium heat. Add the chopped onion and minced garlic, and cook for 2-3 minutes until softened and fragrant.
3. Add the ground turkey to the skillet and cook, breaking it apart with a spoon, until browned and cooked through.
4. Stir in the Italian seasoning, paprika, salt, and pepper, and cook for an additional minute to let the flavors meld.
5. Remove the skillet from the heat and stir in the cooked rice and half of the shredded cheese until well combined.
6. Spoon the turkey and rice mixture evenly into each bell pepper half, pressing down gently to fill them.
7. Sprinkle the remaining shredded cheese over the tops of the stuffed bell peppers.
8. Cover the baking dish with aluminum foil and bake in the preheated oven for 25-30 minutes, or until the bell peppers are tender and the cheese is melted and bubbly.
9. Remove the foil and continue baking for an additional 5-10 minutes to lightly brown the cheese.
10. Remove the stuffed bell peppers from the oven and let them cool for a few minutes before serving.

11. Garnish with chopped fresh parsley or green onions, if desired, before serving.
12. Serve hot and enjoy your delicious stuffed bell peppers with ground turkey and cheese!

These stuffed bell peppers make a hearty and nutritious meal that's perfect for a weeknight dinner or meal prep. Feel free to customize the filling with your favorite ingredients, such as diced tomatoes, black beans, corn, or spices, to suit your taste preferences.

Keto Chocolate Chip Cookies

Ingredients:

- 1 1/2 cups almond flour
- 1/4 cup coconut flour
- 1/2 teaspoon baking soda
- 1/4 teaspoon salt
- 1/2 cup unsalted butter, softened
- 1/2 cup granulated erythritol (or your preferred keto-friendly sweetener)
- 1 large egg
- 1 teaspoon vanilla extract
- 1/2 cup sugar-free chocolate chips

Instructions:

1. Preheat your oven to 350°F (175°C) and line a baking sheet with parchment paper.
2. In a medium bowl, whisk together the almond flour, coconut flour, baking soda, and salt until well combined. Set aside.
3. In a large mixing bowl, cream together the softened butter and granulated erythritol using a hand mixer or stand mixer until light and fluffy.
4. Add the egg and vanilla extract to the butter mixture, and continue mixing until fully combined.
5. Gradually add the dry ingredients to the wet ingredients, mixing on low speed until a dough forms.
6. Fold in the sugar-free chocolate chips until evenly distributed throughout the dough.
7. Use a cookie scoop or spoon to portion out the dough and place it onto the prepared baking sheet, leaving some space between each cookie for spreading.
8. Use your fingers or the back of a spoon to gently flatten each cookie slightly.
9. Bake the cookies in the preheated oven for 10-12 minutes, or until the edges are golden brown.
10. Remove the cookies from the oven and let them cool on the baking sheet for 5 minutes before transferring them to a wire rack to cool completely.
11. Once cooled, store the keto chocolate chip cookies in an airtight container at room temperature for up to 5 days, or in the refrigerator for longer freshness.

12. Enjoy your delicious homemade keto chocolate chip cookies as a satisfying low-carb treat!

These cookies are perfect for anyone following a ketogenic or low-carb diet who still wants to enjoy a sweet treat. They're soft, chewy, and full of chocolatey goodness without all the carbs of traditional cookies.

Creamy Garlic Parmesan Shrimp

Ingredients:

- 1 pound large shrimp, peeled and deveined
- Salt and pepper to taste
- 2 tablespoons olive oil
- 4 cloves garlic, minced
- 1/2 cup chicken broth or white wine
- 1 cup heavy cream
- 1/2 cup grated Parmesan cheese
- 1 teaspoon Italian seasoning
- 2 cups baby spinach leaves
- Fresh parsley, chopped, for garnish (optional)

Instructions:

1. Season the shrimp with salt and pepper to taste.
2. Heat the olive oil in a large skillet over medium heat. Add the minced garlic and cook for 1-2 minutes until fragrant, being careful not to burn it.
3. Add the seasoned shrimp to the skillet and cook for 2-3 minutes on each side until pink and opaque. Remove the shrimp from the skillet and set aside.
4. Deglaze the skillet with chicken broth or white wine, scraping up any browned bits from the bottom of the pan.
5. Stir in the heavy cream, grated Parmesan cheese, and Italian seasoning. Cook for 3-4 minutes, stirring occasionally, until the sauce thickens slightly.
6. Return the cooked shrimp to the skillet and add the baby spinach leaves. Cook for an additional 2-3 minutes, stirring gently, until the spinach wilts and the shrimp is heated through.
7. Taste the sauce and adjust seasoning with salt and pepper if needed.
8. Remove the skillet from the heat and garnish with chopped fresh parsley, if desired.
9. Serve the creamy garlic parmesan shrimp hot, spooned over cooked pasta, rice, or with crusty bread for dipping.
10. Enjoy your delicious and creamy garlic parmesan shrimp!

This dish is perfect for a special dinner or entertaining guests, and it's sure to impress with its rich and indulgent flavors. Feel free to customize the recipe with additional ingredients such as sun-dried tomatoes, mushrooms, or red pepper flakes for a bit of heat.

Taco Stuffed Avocados

Ingredients:

- 2 ripe avocados
- 1/2 pound ground beef or turkey
- 1 tablespoon olive oil
- 1/2 onion, finely chopped
- 2 cloves garlic, minced
- 1 tablespoon taco seasoning
- Salt and pepper to taste
- 1/2 cup diced tomatoes
- 1/4 cup diced red onion
- 1/4 cup shredded cheese (cheddar, Monterey Jack, or your favorite)
- 2 tablespoons chopped fresh cilantro
- Lime wedges, for serving (optional)

Instructions:

1. Cut the avocados in half lengthwise and remove the pits. Scoop out some of the flesh from each avocado half to create a larger cavity for the filling, being careful not to pierce through the skin. Set aside.
2. In a large skillet, heat the olive oil over medium heat. Add the chopped onion and minced garlic, and cook for 2-3 minutes until softened and fragrant.
3. Add the ground beef or turkey to the skillet, breaking it apart with a spoon, and cook until browned and cooked through.
4. Stir in the taco seasoning, salt, and pepper to taste. Cook for an additional minute to let the flavors meld.
5. Remove the skillet from the heat and stir in the diced tomatoes, diced red onion, shredded cheese, and chopped fresh cilantro until well combined.
6. Spoon the taco filling into the cavities of the avocado halves, dividing it evenly among them.
7. Serve the taco stuffed avocados immediately, garnished with additional chopped cilantro and lime wedges on the side for squeezing over the top, if desired.
8. Enjoy your delicious and flavorful taco stuffed avocados!

These taco stuffed avocados are perfect for a quick and satisfying meal that's packed with protein and healthy fats. Feel free to customize the filling with your favorite taco toppings, such as salsa, sour cream, diced jalapeños, or shredded lettuce, to suit your taste preferences.

Spaghetti Squash Carbonara

Ingredients:

- 1 medium spaghetti squash
- 4 slices bacon, chopped
- 2 cloves garlic, minced
- 2 large eggs
- 1/2 cup grated Parmesan cheese
- Salt and black pepper to taste
- Chopped fresh parsley for garnish (optional)

Instructions:

1. Preheat your oven to 400°F (200°C). Line a baking sheet with parchment paper.
2. Cut the spaghetti squash in half lengthwise and scoop out the seeds and stringy bits from the center.
3. Place the squash halves cut side down on the prepared baking sheet. Bake in the preheated oven for 35-45 minutes, or until the squash is tender and easily pierced with a fork.
4. While the squash is baking, cook the chopped bacon in a large skillet over medium heat until crispy. Remove the bacon from the skillet and drain on paper towels, reserving the bacon fat in the skillet.
5. Add the minced garlic to the skillet with the bacon fat and cook for 1-2 minutes until fragrant.
6. In a small bowl, whisk together the eggs and grated Parmesan cheese until smooth. Season with salt and black pepper to taste.
7. Once the spaghetti squash is cooked, remove it from the oven and use a fork to scrape the flesh into spaghetti-like strands.
8. Add the spaghetti squash strands to the skillet with the cooked garlic and bacon fat. Toss to coat the squash in the bacon fat and garlic.
9. Remove the skillet from the heat and quickly pour the egg and Parmesan mixture over the spaghetti squash. Toss everything together until the sauce thickens slightly and coats the squash evenly. The residual heat from the squash will cook the eggs gently.
10. Stir in the cooked bacon pieces.
11. Serve the spaghetti squash carbonara immediately, garnished with chopped fresh parsley if desired.

12. Enjoy your delicious and lighter spaghetti squash carbonara!

This dish is perfect for those looking to cut back on carbs or incorporate more vegetables into their diet. It's rich, creamy, and packed with flavor, making it a satisfying and comforting meal.

Bacon-Wrapped Asparagus

Ingredients:

- 1 pound asparagus spears, woody ends trimmed
- 8-10 slices bacon
- Olive oil (for drizzling)
- Salt and pepper to taste
- Optional: grated Parmesan cheese for garnish

Instructions:

1. Preheat your oven to 400°F (200°C). Line a baking sheet with parchment paper or aluminum foil for easy cleanup.
2. Divide the asparagus spears into bundles of 3-4 spears each, depending on the thickness of the asparagus.
3. Take a slice of bacon and wrap it tightly around each bundle of asparagus, starting from the bottom and wrapping it diagonally to cover as much of the asparagus as possible. Secure the ends of the bacon with toothpicks if needed.
4. Place the bacon-wrapped asparagus bundles on the prepared baking sheet in a single layer.
5. Drizzle olive oil over the bacon-wrapped asparagus bundles and season with salt and pepper to taste.
6. Bake in the preheated oven for 20-25 minutes, or until the bacon is crispy and the asparagus is tender.
7. If desired, sprinkle grated Parmesan cheese over the bacon-wrapped asparagus during the last few minutes of baking, and return to the oven until the cheese is melted and bubbly.
8. Remove the bacon-wrapped asparagus from the oven and let them cool for a few minutes before serving.
9. Serve the bacon-wrapped asparagus as a delicious appetizer or side dish, and enjoy!

This dish is perfect for entertaining or as a special treat for yourself. The combination of crispy bacon and tender asparagus is irresistible, and the simple preparation makes it a go-to recipe for any occasion.

Keto Butter Chicken

Ingredients:

For the marinade:

- 1 pound boneless, skinless chicken thighs or breasts, cut into bite-sized pieces
- 1/4 cup plain Greek yogurt
- 2 tablespoons lemon juice
- 1 tablespoon grated ginger
- 2 cloves garlic, minced
- 1 teaspoon ground turmeric
- 1 teaspoon ground cumin
- 1 teaspoon paprika
- 1/2 teaspoon ground coriander
- 1/2 teaspoon cayenne pepper (adjust to taste)
- Salt and pepper to taste

For the sauce:

- 2 tablespoons butter or ghee
- 1 onion, finely chopped
- 2 cloves garlic, minced
- 1 tablespoon grated ginger
- 1 teaspoon ground turmeric
- 1 teaspoon ground cumin
- 1 teaspoon paprika
- 1/2 teaspoon ground coriander
- 1/2 teaspoon cayenne pepper (adjust to taste)
- 1 cup tomato sauce or crushed tomatoes
- 1/2 cup heavy cream
- Salt and pepper to taste
- Chopped fresh cilantro for garnish (optional)

Instructions:

1. In a bowl, combine the Greek yogurt, lemon juice, grated ginger, minced garlic, ground turmeric, ground cumin, paprika, ground coriander, cayenne pepper, salt, and pepper. Add the chicken pieces and toss to coat. Cover and refrigerate for at least 30 minutes, or up to 24 hours for best flavor.
2. Heat butter or ghee in a large skillet over medium heat. Add the chopped onion and cook until softened, about 5 minutes.
3. Add the minced garlic and grated ginger to the skillet and cook for an additional 1-2 minutes until fragrant.
4. Stir in the ground turmeric, ground cumin, paprika, ground coriander, and cayenne pepper, and cook for another minute to toast the spices.
5. Add the marinated chicken pieces to the skillet, discarding any excess marinade. Cook until the chicken is browned on all sides, about 5-7 minutes.
6. Pour in the tomato sauce or crushed tomatoes and bring to a simmer. Cook for 10-15 minutes, stirring occasionally, until the chicken is cooked through and the sauce has thickened slightly.
7. Stir in the heavy cream and cook for an additional 2-3 minutes until heated through.
8. Taste the sauce and adjust seasoning with salt and pepper as needed.
9. Remove the skillet from the heat and garnish with chopped fresh cilantro, if desired.
10. Serve the keto butter chicken hot, with cauliflower rice or low-carb naan bread on the side, and enjoy!

This keto butter chicken is rich, creamy, and packed with flavor, making it a satisfying and comforting meal for anyone following a low-carb or keto diet. Adjust the level of cayenne pepper to suit your taste preferences, and feel free to customize the dish with additional spices or ingredients as desired.

Broccoli Cheddar Soup

Ingredients:

- 4 tablespoons unsalted butter
- 1 onion, chopped
- 2 cloves garlic, minced
- 1/4 cup all-purpose flour (or almond flour for a low-carb version)
- 4 cups chicken or vegetable broth
- 4 cups chopped fresh broccoli florets
- 1 cup heavy cream (or half-and-half for a lighter version)
- 2 cups shredded cheddar cheese
- Salt and pepper to taste
- Optional toppings: additional shredded cheddar cheese, crumbled cooked bacon, chopped green onions

Instructions:

1. In a large pot or Dutch oven, melt the butter over medium heat. Add the chopped onion and minced garlic, and cook for 3-4 minutes until softened and fragrant.
2. Sprinkle the flour over the onion and garlic mixture, and cook for an additional 1-2 minutes, stirring constantly, to make a roux.
3. Gradually whisk in the chicken or vegetable broth, stirring constantly to prevent lumps from forming.
4. Add the chopped broccoli florets to the pot. Bring the mixture to a simmer, then reduce the heat to low and let it cook for 10-15 minutes, or until the broccoli is tender.
5. Use an immersion blender to puree the soup until smooth and creamy. Alternatively, you can transfer the soup in batches to a blender and blend until smooth, then return it to the pot.
6. Stir in the heavy cream and shredded cheddar cheese until the cheese is melted and the soup is heated through.
7. Season the soup with salt and pepper to taste, adjusting as needed.
8. Ladle the broccoli cheddar soup into bowls and serve hot, garnished with additional shredded cheddar cheese, crumbled cooked bacon, and chopped green onions if desired.
9. Enjoy your delicious and comforting broccoli cheddar soup!

This soup is perfect for a quick and easy weeknight dinner, and it's sure to become a family favorite. Serve it with crusty bread or a side salad for a complete meal, or enjoy it on its own for a cozy and satisfying lunch.

Keto Cheeseburger Casserole

Ingredients:

- 1 pound ground beef
- 1/2 onion, chopped
- 2 cloves garlic, minced
- Salt and pepper to taste
- 1 teaspoon paprika
- 1 teaspoon onion powder
- 1 teaspoon garlic powder
- 1 teaspoon dried mustard powder
- 1/2 cup sugar-free ketchup
- 1/4 cup yellow mustard
- 1 cup shredded cheddar cheese
- 4 large eggs
- 1/4 cup heavy cream or unsweetened almond milk
- Optional toppings: diced tomatoes, chopped pickles, shredded lettuce

Instructions:

1. Preheat your oven to 350°F (175°C). Grease a 9x13-inch baking dish with butter or cooking spray.
2. In a large skillet, cook the ground beef over medium heat until browned and cooked through, breaking it apart with a spoon as it cooks.
3. Add the chopped onion and minced garlic to the skillet with the cooked ground beef. Cook for an additional 2-3 minutes until the onion is softened.
4. Season the ground beef mixture with salt, pepper, paprika, onion powder, garlic powder, and dried mustard powder. Stir to combine.
5. Stir in the sugar-free ketchup and yellow mustard until well combined. Remove the skillet from the heat.
6. Transfer the ground beef mixture to the prepared baking dish and spread it out into an even layer.
7. Sprinkle the shredded cheddar cheese evenly over the top of the ground beef mixture.
8. In a separate bowl, whisk together the eggs and heavy cream or unsweetened almond milk until smooth.
9. Pour the egg mixture evenly over the ground beef and cheese in the baking dish.

10. Bake the casserole in the preheated oven for 25-30 minutes, or until the eggs are set and the top is golden brown.
11. Remove the casserole from the oven and let it cool for a few minutes before slicing.
12. Serve the keto cheeseburger casserole hot, garnished with diced tomatoes, chopped pickles, shredded lettuce, or your favorite burger toppings.
13. Enjoy your delicious and satisfying keto cheeseburger casserole!

This dish is perfect for a quick and easy weeknight dinner or meal prep, and it's sure to be a hit with the whole family. Feel free to customize the toppings to suit your taste preferences, just like you would with a classic cheeseburger.

Creamy Lemon Garlic Chicken

Ingredients:

- 4 boneless, skinless chicken breasts
- Salt and pepper to taste
- 2 tablespoons olive oil
- 4 cloves garlic, minced
- 1 cup chicken broth
- 1/2 cup heavy cream
- Zest of 1 lemon
- Juice of 1 lemon
- 2 tablespoons unsalted butter
- 2 tablespoons chopped fresh parsley
- Lemon slices for garnish (optional)

Instructions:

1. Season the chicken breasts with salt and pepper on both sides.
2. In a large skillet, heat the olive oil over medium-high heat. Add the chicken breasts to the skillet and cook for 5-7 minutes on each side, or until golden brown and cooked through. Remove the chicken from the skillet and set aside.
3. In the same skillet, add the minced garlic and cook for 1-2 minutes until fragrant.
4. Pour the chicken broth into the skillet, scraping up any browned bits from the bottom of the pan.
5. Stir in the heavy cream, lemon zest, and lemon juice. Bring the mixture to a simmer and cook for 2-3 minutes to thicken slightly.
6. Reduce the heat to low and stir in the unsalted butter until melted and the sauce is smooth.
7. Return the cooked chicken breasts to the skillet, spooning the sauce over the top. Simmer for an additional 2-3 minutes to heat the chicken through.
8. Garnish the creamy lemon garlic chicken with chopped fresh parsley and lemon slices, if desired.
9. Serve hot, spooning the creamy sauce over the chicken breasts.
10. Enjoy your creamy lemon garlic chicken with your favorite side dishes, such as rice, pasta, or steamed vegetables.

This dish is perfect for a special dinner or entertaining guests, and it's sure to impress with its vibrant flavors and elegant presentation. Adjust the amount of lemon juice and garlic to suit your taste preferences, and feel free to add additional herbs or spices for extra flavor.

Avocado Tuna Salad

Ingredients:

- 2 cans (5 ounces each) tuna, drained
- 1 ripe avocado, peeled and diced
- 1/4 cup diced red onion
- 1/4 cup diced celery
- 1/4 cup diced red bell pepper
- 2 tablespoons chopped fresh parsley or cilantro
- 2 tablespoons mayonnaise
- 1 tablespoon lemon juice
- Salt and pepper to taste
- Optional add-ins: diced cucumber, chopped pickles, sliced olives

Instructions:

1. In a large mixing bowl, combine the drained tuna, diced avocado, diced red onion, diced celery, diced red bell pepper, and chopped fresh parsley or cilantro.
2. In a small bowl, whisk together the mayonnaise and lemon juice until smooth.
3. Pour the mayonnaise mixture over the tuna and avocado mixture in the large bowl.
4. Gently toss everything together until well combined, being careful not to mash the avocado too much.
5. Season the avocado tuna salad with salt and pepper to taste, and adjust seasoning as needed.
6. If desired, add optional add-ins such as diced cucumber, chopped pickles, or sliced olives, and stir to incorporate.
7. Serve the avocado tuna salad immediately, or refrigerate for 30 minutes to allow the flavors to meld before serving.
8. Enjoy your creamy and flavorful avocado tuna salad as a filling for sandwiches, wraps, or lettuce cups, or simply enjoy it on its own as a light and healthy meal.

This avocado tuna salad is versatile and customizable, making it perfect for meal prep, picnics, or quick and easy lunches. Feel free to adjust the ingredients and seasonings to suit your taste preferences, and add your favorite mix-ins for extra texture and flavor.

Almond Flour Blueberry Muffins

Ingredients:

- 2 cups almond flour
- 1/4 cup granulated erythritol (or your preferred sweetener)
- 1 teaspoon baking powder
- 1/4 teaspoon salt
- 3 large eggs
- 1/4 cup unsweetened almond milk (or any milk of your choice)
- 1/4 cup melted coconut oil (or melted butter)
- 1 teaspoon vanilla extract
- 1 cup fresh or frozen blueberries

Instructions:

1. Preheat your oven to 350°F (175°C). Line a muffin tin with paper liners or grease the cups with cooking spray.
2. In a large mixing bowl, whisk together the almond flour, granulated erythritol, baking powder, and salt until well combined.
3. In a separate bowl, whisk together the eggs, almond milk, melted coconut oil, and vanilla extract until smooth.
4. Pour the wet ingredients into the dry ingredients and stir until just combined. Be careful not to overmix.
5. Gently fold in the blueberries until evenly distributed throughout the batter.
6. Divide the batter evenly among the muffin cups, filling each cup about 2/3 full.
7. Bake in the preheated oven for 20-25 minutes, or until the muffins are golden brown and a toothpick inserted into the center comes out clean.
8. Remove the muffins from the oven and let them cool in the muffin tin for 5 minutes before transferring them to a wire rack to cool completely.
9. Enjoy your almond flour blueberry muffins warm or at room temperature.

These muffins are naturally gluten-free, low-carb, and packed with almond flour's nutty goodness. They're perfect for anyone looking for a healthier alternative to traditional muffins. Feel free to customize the recipe by adding chopped nuts, cinnamon, or lemon zest for extra flavor.

Bacon-Wrapped Jalapeno Poppers

Ingredients:

- 12 jalapeño peppers
- 8 ounces cream cheese, softened
- 1/2 cup shredded cheddar cheese
- 1/2 teaspoon garlic powder
- 1/2 teaspoon onion powder
- Salt and pepper to taste
- 12 slices bacon, cut in half crosswise
- Toothpicks

Instructions:

1. Preheat your oven to 400°F (200°C). Line a baking sheet with aluminum foil and place a wire rack on top.
2. Cut the jalapeño peppers in half lengthwise and use a spoon to scoop out the seeds and membranes, creating little pepper boats.
3. In a mixing bowl, combine the softened cream cheese, shredded cheddar cheese, garlic powder, onion powder, salt, and pepper. Mix until well combined.
4. Spoon the cream cheese mixture into each jalapeño half, filling them to the top.
5. Wrap each stuffed jalapeño half with a half-slice of bacon, securing it in place with a toothpick. Repeat with all the jalapeño halves.
6. Place the bacon-wrapped jalapeño poppers on the wire rack on the prepared baking sheet.
7. Bake in the preheated oven for 20-25 minutes, or until the bacon is crispy and the jalapeños are tender.
8. Remove the jalapeño poppers from the oven and let them cool for a few minutes before serving.
9. Serve the bacon-wrapped jalapeño poppers warm as a delicious appetizer or snack.

These bacon-wrapped jalapeño poppers are perfect for parties, game day gatherings, or any occasion where you want to serve up some spicy, cheesy goodness. Feel free to adjust the level of heat by removing some or all of the seeds and membranes from the jalapeños, or by using a milder pepper variety if desired. Enjoy!

Keto Chicken Salad Lettuce Wraps

Ingredients:

For the chicken salad:

- 2 cups cooked chicken breast, shredded or diced
- 1/4 cup mayonnaise
- 2 tablespoons Greek yogurt (or sour cream)
- 1 tablespoon Dijon mustard
- 1 celery stalk, finely diced
- 2 green onions, thinly sliced
- 1/4 cup chopped fresh parsley
- Salt and pepper to taste

For serving:

- Large lettuce leaves (such as Bibb, butter, or romaine)
- Optional toppings: sliced avocado, chopped tomatoes, cooked bacon bits

Instructions:

1. In a large mixing bowl, combine the cooked chicken breast, mayonnaise, Greek yogurt, Dijon mustard, diced celery, sliced green onions, and chopped fresh parsley.
2. Stir the ingredients together until well combined and the chicken is evenly coated with the dressing. Season with salt and pepper to taste.
3. To assemble the lettuce wraps, place a spoonful of the chicken salad mixture onto the center of each lettuce leaf.
4. Add any optional toppings you like, such as sliced avocado, chopped tomatoes, or cooked bacon bits.
5. Fold the sides of the lettuce leaf over the filling, then roll it up tightly to create a wrap.
6. Repeat with the remaining lettuce leaves and chicken salad mixture.
7. Serve the keto chicken salad lettuce wraps immediately, or refrigerate them for later.

These lettuce wraps are perfect for a light and satisfying meal that's packed with protein and healthy fats. They're customizable, so feel free to add your favorite low-carb ingredients to suit your taste preferences. Enjoy!

Cheesy Cauliflower Breadsticks

Ingredients:

- 1 medium head of cauliflower, cut into florets
- 2 large eggs
- 1 cup shredded mozzarella cheese
- 1/4 cup grated Parmesan cheese
- 1 teaspoon Italian seasoning
- 1/2 teaspoon garlic powder
- Salt and pepper to taste
- Marinara sauce for dipping (optional)

Instructions:

1. Preheat your oven to 425°F (220°C). Line a baking sheet with parchment paper.
2. Place the cauliflower florets in a food processor and pulse until they resemble fine crumbs, similar to rice or couscous.
3. Transfer the cauliflower crumbs to a microwave-safe bowl and microwave on high for 4-5 minutes, or until softened. Let cool slightly.
4. Once the cauliflower has cooled, place it in a clean kitchen towel or cheesecloth and squeeze out as much excess moisture as possible. This step is important to ensure the breadsticks hold together well.
5. In a large mixing bowl, combine the squeezed cauliflower, eggs, shredded mozzarella cheese, grated Parmesan cheese, Italian seasoning, garlic powder, salt, and pepper. Mix until well combined.
6. Transfer the cauliflower mixture to the prepared baking sheet and spread it out into a rectangle, about 1/4 inch thick.
7. Bake in the preheated oven for 20-25 minutes, or until the edges are golden brown and the breadsticks are firm to the touch.
8. Remove the baking sheet from the oven and let the cauliflower breadsticks cool for a few minutes.
9. Using a sharp knife, cut the cauliflower breadsticks into strips to resemble breadsticks.
10. Serve the cheesy cauliflower breadsticks warm, with marinara sauce for dipping if desired.

These cheesy cauliflower breadsticks are a tasty and satisfying snack or side dish that's perfect for anyone following a low-carb or gluten-free diet. They're packed with flavor and cheesy goodness, making them a hit with the whole family. Enjoy!

Grilled Lemon Herb Chicken

Ingredients:

- 4 boneless, skinless chicken breasts
- 2 lemons, juiced and zested
- 2 cloves garlic, minced
- 2 tablespoons olive oil
- 1 tablespoon fresh chopped herbs (such as rosemary, thyme, or oregano)
- Salt and pepper to taste

Instructions:

1. In a small bowl, whisk together the lemon juice, lemon zest, minced garlic, olive oil, chopped herbs, salt, and pepper to make the marinade.
2. Place the chicken breasts in a shallow dish or resealable plastic bag and pour the marinade over them, making sure they are well coated. Marinate the chicken in the refrigerator for at least 30 minutes, or up to 4 hours for best flavor.
3. Preheat your grill to medium-high heat. Make sure the grates are clean and lightly oiled to prevent sticking.
4. Remove the chicken breasts from the marinade and discard any excess marinade.
5. Grill the chicken breasts for 6-8 minutes per side, or until they are cooked through and have reached an internal temperature of 165°F (75°C). The cooking time will vary depending on the thickness of the chicken breasts.
6. Once the chicken is cooked through, remove it from the grill and let it rest for a few minutes before serving.
7. Serve the grilled lemon herb chicken hot, garnished with additional lemon slices and chopped herbs if desired.
8. Enjoy your flavorful and juicy grilled lemon herb chicken!

This dish pairs well with a variety of side dishes, such as grilled vegetables, rice, quinoa, or a fresh salad. The combination of zesty lemon, fragrant herbs, and tender chicken makes for a delightful and satisfying meal that's sure to be a hit with your family and friends.

Keto Chocolate Peanut Butter Fat Bombs

Ingredients:

- 1/2 cup natural peanut butter (sugar-free)
- 1/4 cup coconut oil, melted
- 2 tablespoons unsweetened cocoa powder
- 2 tablespoons powdered erythritol or another keto-friendly sweetener, to taste
- 1/2 teaspoon vanilla extract
- Pinch of salt (optional)

Instructions:

1. In a mixing bowl, combine the melted coconut oil and natural peanut butter. Stir until smooth and well combined.
2. Add the unsweetened cocoa powder, powdered erythritol, vanilla extract, and a pinch of salt if desired. Mix until all ingredients are fully incorporated and the mixture is smooth.
3. Taste the mixture and adjust the sweetness to your liking by adding more powdered erythritol if needed.
4. Spoon the mixture into silicone molds or mini muffin cups lined with paper liners, filling each mold or cup about halfway full.
5. Place the molds or muffin cups in the freezer and chill for at least 30 minutes, or until the fat bombs are firm and set.
6. Once firm, remove the fat bombs from the molds or muffin cups and store them in an airtight container in the refrigerator or freezer until ready to eat.
7. Enjoy your keto chocolate peanut butter fat bombs as a delicious and satisfying treat!

These fat bombs are perfect for satisfying your sweet cravings while staying on track with your keto diet. They're rich, creamy, and packed with flavor, making them a delightful snack or dessert option. Feel free to customize the recipe by adding chopped nuts or a sprinkle of sea salt on top for extra texture and flavor.

Creamy Mushroom Risotto

Ingredients:

- 1 cup Arborio rice (risotto rice)
- 4 cups chicken or vegetable broth
- 2 tablespoons olive oil
- 1 tablespoon butter
- 1 onion, finely chopped
- 2 cloves garlic, minced
- 8 ounces mushrooms (such as cremini or button mushrooms), sliced
- 1/2 cup dry white wine (optional)
- 1/2 cup grated Parmesan cheese
- Salt and pepper to taste
- Chopped fresh parsley for garnish (optional)

Instructions:

1. In a medium saucepan, heat the chicken or vegetable broth over medium heat until hot. Reduce the heat to low and keep the broth warm while you prepare the risotto.
2. In a large skillet or saucepan, heat the olive oil and butter over medium heat. Add the chopped onion and cook until softened, about 3-4 minutes.
3. Add the minced garlic to the skillet and cook for an additional 1-2 minutes until fragrant.
4. Add the sliced mushrooms to the skillet and cook until they are golden brown and tender, about 5-6 minutes.
5. Add the Arborio rice to the skillet and cook, stirring constantly, for 1-2 minutes until the rice is well coated with the oil and begins to turn translucent around the edges.
6. If using, pour in the white wine and cook, stirring constantly, until the wine is absorbed by the rice.
7. Begin adding the warm chicken or vegetable broth to the skillet, one ladleful at a time, stirring constantly and allowing each addition of broth to be absorbed before adding more. Continue this process until the rice is creamy and tender, but still slightly al dente, about 18-20 minutes. You may not need to use all of the broth.

8. Stir in the grated Parmesan cheese until melted and well combined. Season the risotto with salt and pepper to taste.
9. Remove the skillet from the heat and let the risotto rest for a few minutes.
10. Serve the creamy mushroom risotto hot, garnished with chopped fresh parsley if desired.

This creamy mushroom risotto is rich, flavorful, and comforting, making it perfect for a special dinner or entertaining guests. Serve it as a side dish or as a main course, accompanied by a green salad or roasted vegetables. Enjoy!

Sausage and Pepperoni Cauliflower Pizza Casserole

Ingredients:

- 1 medium head of cauliflower, cut into florets
- 1 tablespoon olive oil
- 1/2 teaspoon Italian seasoning
- Salt and pepper to taste
- 1/2 cup pizza sauce
- 1 cup shredded mozzarella cheese
- 1/4 cup grated Parmesan cheese
- 4 ounces cooked Italian sausage, crumbled
- 2 ounces pepperoni slices
- 1/4 cup sliced black olives (optional)
- Fresh basil leaves for garnish (optional)

Instructions:

1. Preheat your oven to 400°F (200°C). Grease a 9x13-inch baking dish with olive oil or cooking spray.
2. Place the cauliflower florets in a large mixing bowl. Drizzle with olive oil and sprinkle with Italian seasoning, salt, and pepper. Toss until the cauliflower is evenly coated.
3. Spread the cauliflower in an even layer in the prepared baking dish.
4. Bake in the preheated oven for 15-20 minutes, or until the cauliflower is tender and lightly browned.
5. Remove the baking dish from the oven and spread the pizza sauce evenly over the roasted cauliflower.
6. Sprinkle the shredded mozzarella cheese and grated Parmesan cheese over the pizza sauce.
7. Scatter the crumbled Italian sausage, pepperoni slices, and sliced black olives (if using) over the cheese.
8. Return the baking dish to the oven and bake for an additional 10-15 minutes, or until the cheese is melted and bubbly.
9. Remove the cauliflower pizza casserole from the oven and let it cool for a few minutes before slicing.
10. Garnish with fresh basil leaves before serving, if desired.

11. Serve the sausage and pepperoni cauliflower pizza casserole hot, as a delicious and satisfying low-carb meal.

This cauliflower pizza casserole is packed with flavor and makes for a hearty and comforting dish that's perfect for a cozy dinner or entertaining guests. Feel free to customize the toppings to suit your taste preferences, adding any of your favorite pizza toppings such as bell peppers, onions, or mushrooms. Enjoy!

Lemon Butter Salmon

Ingredients:

- 4 salmon fillets, skin-on or skinless, about 6 ounces each
- Salt and pepper to taste
- 2 tablespoons olive oil
- 4 tablespoons unsalted butter
- 2 cloves garlic, minced
- Zest and juice of 1 lemon
- 2 tablespoons chopped fresh parsley
- Lemon slices for garnish (optional)

Instructions:

1. Pat the salmon fillets dry with paper towels and season both sides with salt and pepper to taste.
2. In a large skillet, heat the olive oil over medium-high heat. Once hot, add the salmon fillets to the skillet, skin-side down if using skin-on fillets.
3. Cook the salmon for 3-4 minutes on the first side, then carefully flip each fillet using a spatula. Cook for an additional 3-4 minutes on the second side, or until the salmon is cooked to your desired level of doneness. The salmon should be opaque and flake easily with a fork.
4. Transfer the cooked salmon fillets to a plate and cover loosely with foil to keep warm.
5. In the same skillet, reduce the heat to medium-low and add the unsalted butter. Once melted, add the minced garlic and cook for 1-2 minutes until fragrant, being careful not to let it burn.
6. Add the lemon zest and lemon juice to the skillet, stirring to combine with the butter and garlic.
7. Stir in the chopped fresh parsley and season the lemon butter sauce with salt and pepper to taste.
8. Spoon the lemon butter sauce over the cooked salmon fillets, coating them evenly.
9. Garnish the lemon butter salmon with lemon slices if desired, and serve hot.

This lemon butter salmon is a delicious and nutritious dish that's perfect for a special dinner or entertaining guests. Serve it with your favorite side dishes, such as steamed vegetables, rice, or a fresh salad, for a complete meal. Enjoy!

Chicken Bacon Ranch Casserole

Ingredients:

- 4 cups cooked and shredded chicken breasts (about 2-3 breasts)
- 8 slices bacon, cooked until crispy and crumbled
- 1 cup ranch dressing (homemade or store-bought)
- 1 cup shredded cheddar cheese
- 1 cup shredded mozzarella cheese
- 1/4 cup chopped green onions (optional)
- Salt and pepper to taste
- Chopped fresh parsley for garnish (optional)

Instructions:

1. Preheat your oven to 375°F (190°C). Grease a 9x13-inch baking dish with cooking spray or butter.
2. In a large mixing bowl, combine the cooked and shredded chicken breasts with the crumbled bacon.
3. Add the ranch dressing to the bowl and toss until the chicken and bacon are evenly coated.
4. Stir in the shredded cheddar cheese and shredded mozzarella cheese until well combined. Season with salt and pepper to taste.
5. Transfer the chicken bacon ranch mixture to the prepared baking dish and spread it out into an even layer.
6. Bake in the preheated oven for 20-25 minutes, or until the cheese is melted and bubbly and the casserole is heated through.
7. Remove the casserole from the oven and sprinkle the chopped green onions over the top, if using.
8. Garnish the chicken bacon ranch casserole with chopped fresh parsley for a pop of color and freshness, if desired.
9. Serve the casserole hot, spooning it onto plates or into bowls.

This chicken bacon ranch casserole is a comforting and satisfying meal that's perfect for a cozy dinner or feeding a crowd. It's easy to make and packed with delicious flavors that everyone will love. Enjoy!

Keto Strawberry Cheesecake Bites

Ingredients:

- 8 ounces cream cheese, softened
- 1/4 cup powdered erythritol or another keto-friendly sweetener
- 1 teaspoon vanilla extract
- 1/4 cup heavy cream
- 8-10 fresh strawberries, hulled and halved

Instructions:

1. In a mixing bowl, beat the softened cream cheese until smooth and creamy.
2. Add the powdered erythritol and vanilla extract to the cream cheese, and beat until well combined and smooth.
3. In a separate mixing bowl, whip the heavy cream until stiff peaks form.
4. Gently fold the whipped cream into the cream cheese mixture until fully incorporated.
5. Spoon or pipe the cheesecake mixture into the halved strawberries, filling each strawberry generously.
6. Place the filled strawberries on a serving platter or tray.
7. Optional: Refrigerate the filled strawberries for 30 minutes to allow the cheesecake filling to set.
8. Serve the keto strawberry cheesecake bites immediately, or store them in the refrigerator until ready to serve.

These keto strawberry cheesecake bites are a delightful and satisfying treat that's perfect for satisfying your sweet cravings while staying on track with your low-carb lifestyle. Enjoy!

Spicy Thai Coconut Soup

Ingredients:

- 1 tablespoon coconut oil or vegetable oil
- 1 small onion, finely chopped
- 2 cloves garlic, minced
- 1 tablespoon fresh ginger, grated
- 2 tablespoons Thai red curry paste
- 4 cups chicken broth
- 1 can (13.5 ounces) coconut milk
- 1 tablespoon fish sauce
- 1 tablespoon soy sauce (or tamari for gluten-free)
- 1 tablespoon brown sugar or coconut sugar
- 1 stalk lemongrass, bruised and cut into pieces
- 2 kaffir lime leaves (optional)
- 2 cups cooked chicken breast, shredded or diced
- 1 cup mushrooms, sliced
- 1 red bell pepper, thinly sliced
- 1 tablespoon lime juice
- Salt and pepper to taste
- Fresh cilantro leaves for garnish
- Thai basil leaves for garnish (optional)
- Sliced red chili for garnish (optional)

Instructions:

1. In a large pot or Dutch oven, heat the coconut oil over medium heat. Add the chopped onion, minced garlic, and grated ginger, and sauté until fragrant, about 2-3 minutes.
2. Add the Thai red curry paste to the pot and stir to combine with the aromatics. Cook for an additional 1-2 minutes to toast the curry paste and enhance its flavor.
3. Pour in the chicken broth and coconut milk, stirring well to combine. Add the fish sauce, soy sauce, and brown sugar (or coconut sugar) to the pot, and stir until the sugar is dissolved.
4. Add the bruised lemongrass stalk and kaffir lime leaves (if using) to the pot, and bring the soup to a simmer. Let it simmer gently for about 10 minutes to allow the flavors to meld together.

5. Stir in the cooked chicken breast, sliced mushrooms, and thinly sliced red bell pepper. Simmer for an additional 5-7 minutes, or until the vegetables are tender and the chicken is heated through.
6. Remove the pot from the heat and discard the lemongrass stalk and kaffir lime leaves.
7. Stir in the lime juice, and season the soup with salt and pepper to taste.
8. Ladle the spicy Thai coconut soup into serving bowls, and garnish with fresh cilantro leaves, Thai basil leaves (if using), and sliced red chili for added heat (if desired).
9. Serve the soup hot as a delicious and comforting meal.

This spicy Thai coconut soup is packed with aromatic flavors and creamy coconut goodness, making it a satisfying and warming dish that's perfect for any occasion. Enjoy!